17.98

SCOTTISH ISLANDS

SCOTTISH ISLANDS

Charlie Waite

Constable · London

First published in Great Britain 1989
by Constable and Company Limited
10 Orange Street London WC2H 7EG
Copyright © 1989 text and photographs
by Charlie Waite
Set in Monophoto Photina 11pt by
BAS Printers Limited, Over Wallop, Hampshire
Printed and bound in Great Britain by
Richard Clay Limited, Bungay, Suffolk

British Library CIP data
Waite, Charlie, *1949–*
Scottish islands
1. Scotland. Hebrides. Description & travel
I. Title
914.11′4858

ISBN 0-09-467570-8

For Romilly, Kaia, Leah,
and all that is Braad

INTRODUCTION

On my first visit to the Scottish islands, I heard an elderly American visitor, looking around her, remark complacently: 'It's all very low key compared to New York!'

And indeed it is. The islanders thrive on isolation rather than crowds. Separated by vast stretches of ocean, the small communities feel no need to visit one another, let alone the Scottish mainland. The islands are often flat and featureless rather than packed with novelty at every step. Fuel is still predominantly peat, rather than oil. There are only two industries, if they can be so called: sheep and salmon. The people are all crofters, and their lives need endurance and fortitude of quite a different kind from that demanded by living in the concrete canyons of New York City.

My first visit to any of the islands was a quick trip to Skye some ten years ago. Like any other tourist I saw the 'sights' – the stupendous Cuillin Mountains, the Old Man of Storr, the bulk of Quiraing jutting up from the empty moorland round it. Mountains are exciting and dramatic, and immediately overawe the onlooker. I was prepared for this by all that I'd seen or read of Skye: I was keyed up to respond to that kind of beauty.

But the beauty of the Scottish islands in general is quite different. The Inner Hebrides – Mull, Iona, Arran and Islay – though less dramatic than Skye itself, still are more mountainous than the Outer Hebrides, and have trees growing on them – even some forests. Though lonely and often austere, they did not fully prepare me for Coll, North and South Uist, Harris, and Lewis. Physically remote, barren and flat, the Outer Hebrides take the brunt of the bad weather, and the gales and storms that sweep over them from the Atlantic seem to have blown away most of their features. I found them forbidding, even frightening. Their beauty does not instantly strike the eye, for they are in every way, as the American lady said, low key. Coll, in particular, seemed to me at first view inhospitable to the point of hostility. Nothing except a desert could contrast more strongly with the varied, cosy prettiness of the English countryside, or the turbulent streets of any city.

It takes time to appreciate the Scottish islands, time to shed the need for hustle and bustle, to slow down, to look and start to see. The subtlety of light and shadow. The shapes of the rocks, still surprisingly sharp and jagged despite the scouring of wind and water down the centuries. The colour of lichens. The curve of a hillside. Cloudscapes. The shimmer of water.

Nowhere in the world have I been so aware of water. There are pools, lochs and lochans in their hundreds. Some, higher up, are freshwater, filled by the rain. Others, though apparently far inland, are salty, for they curve and snake across the tundra and eventually link up with the sea. Almost all are peaty, coloured a deep chocolate brown that seems not to reflect light but rather to absorb it. And of course there is always the sea, circling each island. After the still and sombre lochans, it comes almost as a suprise to see the water moving, crashing and thundering on the empty beaches. On fine days the sea can look like the Caribbean, so blue that the colour is almost crude, but in stormy weather it is terrifying.

From the photographer's point of view, bad weather means flat light, no shadow, and thus no awareness of dimension, which is restricting. In the Hebrides one is very aware of the weather, constantly looking up at the sky to see what one is in for! Often the clouds hang so low and heavy with water that you feel nothing could ever shift them. They will latch on to a mountain top, say, and persist there for days. But when the wind gets up, they move so quickly across the immense arch of the sky that you can look across the tundra and chase after the light you want. Taking pictures in such conditions is great fun. You can 'place' your light in the foreground or else striking a hillside in the distance, by waiting for the rapidly moving clouds to pass or by driving a few miles in your car and leaving a patch of mist and squall behind.

Pure blue sky, in fact, is the enemy of the photographer. Sky forms about a third of a picture, and no artist would chooose to paint that much of his canvas a solid blue. Yet on a fine day that is what the photographer is landed with. The alternative then is to choose to photograph details – the shape of a rock, an upturned boat, a pattern of sand and pebbles – and exclude the sky altogether.

The colours of the Scottish islands are muted on the whole – watercolours, so to speak, rather than oils. For photography, this is a bonus. Bright primary colours, however true to life, are tainted by the suggestion of 'chocolate box' pictures. Good pictures are about components and ingredients, about selection. Too much information – and strong colours are part of that information – makes a picture harder for the viewer to assimilate and respond to. Subtle blending of shades, approaching monochrome sometimes, lends itself to better photographs.

The problem of photographing landscape is one of conveying emotion. The person seeing the landscape, the magnificent vista, is filled with the romanticism and beauty of the scene, and reaches for his camera to capture it. But the camera has no emotion, it is purely a machine. We all hurry back from holiday, excited by the prospect of developing holiday pictures, and then are disappointed when we collect them from the chemist. That great, big, wonderful view looks strangely flat and lifeless, arousing none of the ecstasy in our friends at home that it did in us when we saw it. For the photographer cannot casually assume that the beauty in front of him will result in a beautiful picture. The secret is to be selective, to reduce the elements in a photograph to the minimum, to two or three at most – to concentrate the flavour, as it were, by dwelling on the essential ingredients.

I was fascinated by the Hebrides and disturbed by them, in almost equal parts. I liked the emptiness of the Outer Islands, knowing as I looked across the tundra of Coll that possibly nobody had walked across it for years. There are no mountains to be climbed on the far side, no point in trudging through the heather: the few people there – crofters and fishermen – stick to the roads. I liked the way the birds were almost fearless. They are so seldom disturbed that I could often get very close to them. The silence was wonderful – even on on windy days the wind is almost noiseless because of the lack of trees and vegetation.

My favourite photographic maxim is that of Ansel Adams: 'Chance favours the prepared mind.' If you are highly tuned and 'on the hunt', you'll be receptive to anything that is in your style. Your eye will make connections, will leap to the key element of a scene, to the small but telling detail. In the Scottish islands – silent, lonely, open to the immense sky, with only sheep, rocks, birds and flowers for company – I found the perfect conditions for sharpening my perceptions and opening my mind in this way.

C.W.

1989

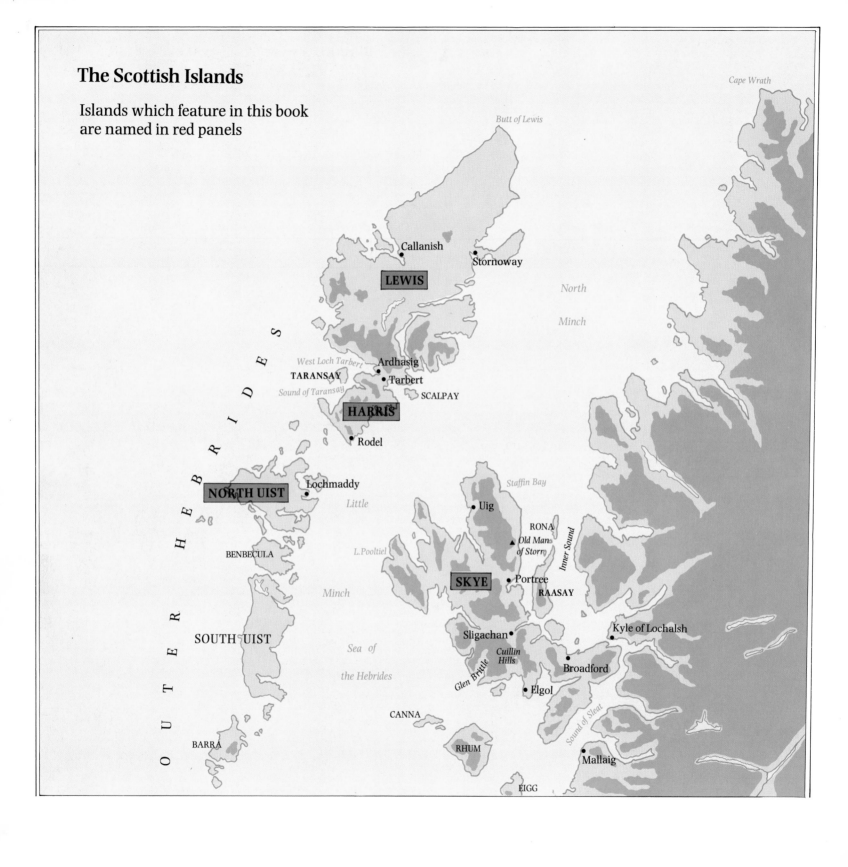

The Scottish Islands

Islands which feature in this book
are named in red panels

Cape Wrath

Butt of Lewis

Callanish

Stornoway

LEWIS

North

Minch

West Loch Tarbert

Ardhasig

TARANSAY

Tarbert

Sound of Taransay

SCALPAY

HARRIS

Rodel

NORTH UIST

Lochmaddy

Little

Staffin Bay

Uig

RONA

Old Man
of Storr

Inner Sound

BENBECULA

L. Pooltiel

SKYE

Portree

RAASAY

Minch

Kyle of Lochalsh

SOUTH UIST

Sligachan

Cuillin
Hills

Broadford

Sea of

Glen Brittle

Elgol

the Hebrides

CANNA

CANNA

BARRA

RHUM

Mallaig

Sound of Sleat

EIGG

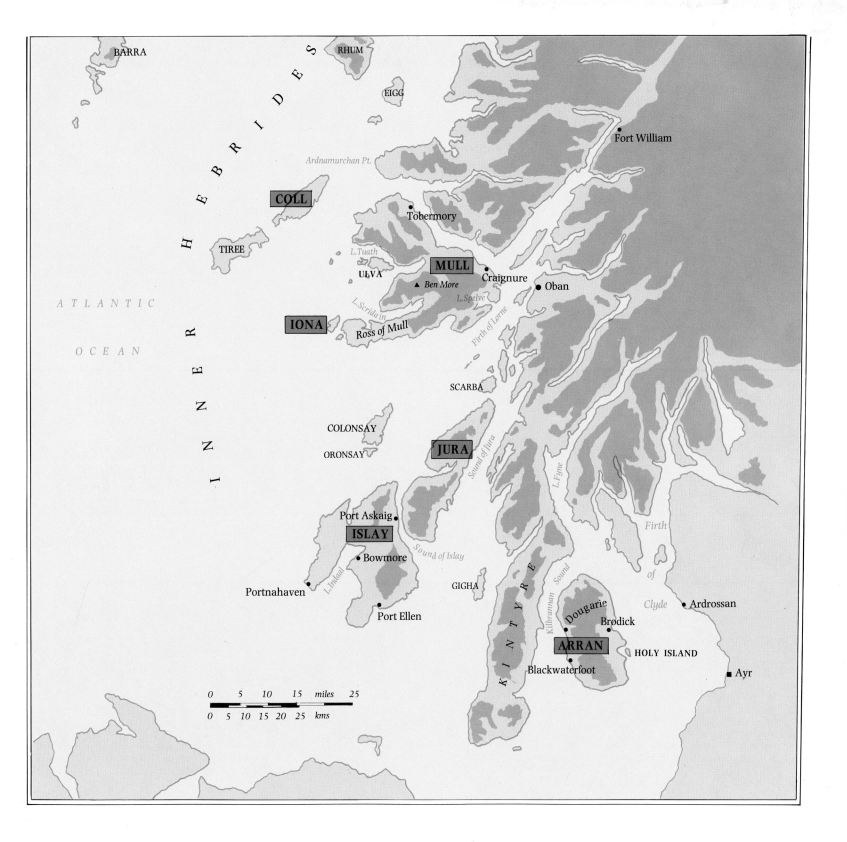

BARRA

RHUM

EIGG

H E B R I D E S

Fort William

Ardnamurchan Pt.

COLL

Tobermory

TIREE

L.Tuath

ULVA

MULL

Craignure

Oban

▲ *Ben More*

L.Scridain

L.Spelve

A T L A N T I C

IONA

Ross of Mull

Firth of Lorne

O C E A N

I N N E R

SCARBA

COLONSAY

JURA

ORONSAY

JURA

Sound of Jura

L.Fyne

Port Askaig

Firth

ISLAY

of

Bowmore

Sound of Islay

Clyde

Ardrossan

Portnahaven

L.Indaal

GIGHA

Dougarie

Port Ellen

K I N T Y R E

Kilbrannan Sound

Brodick

ARRAN

HOLY ISLAND

Blackwaterfoot

Ayr

0   5   10   15   *miles*   25

0   5 10 15 20 25   *kms*

ARRAN

(1) Holy Island, in the Firth of Clyde, is seen here from Arran across the sands of Lamlash Bay. The abundant wildlife on Holy Island is seldom disturbed by human intruders.

_____

(2) This view from Brodick, across an often tranquil bay, has the famous peak of Goat Fell on the skyline.

(3) This could, perhaps, be imagined to be a land mass as seen from the air – in fact it shows the fascinating patterns on a rock, on the shore near Brodick.

(4) On the same shore as the previous picture
– a round, lichen-covered football of a rock
nestles among larger boulders.

_____

(5) North of Brodick, the late evening sun casts fingers of shadow on the rippled sand. In the distance, to the south-east, can be seen the peak of Holy Island.

(6) Cioch-na-h-Oigh, north of Brodick – the splendid Goat Fell, climbed by so many visitors, lies out of the photograph to the left of this tranquil valley.

(7) The stones on the beach near Dougarie are
sculptured by the weather, so that every one
offers a comfortable seat. The view is across
Kilbrannan Sound to the island of Kintyre.

(8) Iorsa Water flows into Kilbrannan Sound at Dougarie – this is the last opportunity to drink from the sweet-tasting river before it enters the salt waters of the Sound.

(9) The Scottish islands are famous for their whisky, their beauty – and for their magnificent sunsets, as any islander living on the western shore will confirm. In this picture, taken near Dougarie, the sun sets over Kintyre.

(10) The western shore of Arran, around Whitefarland Point, offers some of the island's best grazing land. The low bulk of Kintyre lies across Kilbrannan Sound.

(11) This solitary standing stone is at Auchencar, north of Blackwaterfoot. There are many such on the Isle of Arran, and no authentic explanation is attached to any of them.

ISLAY

(12) Claggain Bay, in the south-east of the
island: it is unusual to see a swan in such a
vast expanse of sea-water, and entirely alone.

(13) This wind-bent tree stands on the shores
of Claggain Bay: trees on the shores of any
Scottish island are seldom vertical.

(14) The mighty Paps of Jura are the highest
hills on that island, which is only a few
minutes by boat from Islay. They are seen here
from Port Askaig: there are in fact three Paps
but only two are visible from this viewpoint.
Rarely do they shed their veiling of cloud,
which here is coloured by the setting sun.

(15) Loch Indaal is a great scoop of a bay on the north-west coast of Islay. Often as many as five hundred sheep congregate on the sand here, which results in some overcrowding.

(16) Cattle as well as sheep gather together on the shore of Loch Indaal, almost as if to exchange gossip.

(17) Portnahaven is on the extreme
westernmost tip of Islay, jutting out into the
ocean. This little church at Portnahaven
stands alone in a field which in spring is a
mass of wild flowers.

(18) Cattle paddling in the shallow waters of
Loch Indaal: they are photographed from
Bridgend, at the head of the bay.

(19) This peaceful scene is photographed from Bowmore on the southern shore of Loch Indaal, looking north towards Bruichladdich. After a storm the sky presented this stunning arrangement of cloud and sunlight.

(20) Bowmore: the last stone house at the edge of the loch stands at the end of a perfectly straight street.

JURA

(21) Photographed near Lagg Bay, this is one of the few trees on the island. Poor soil and fierce weather allow them only a short life.

MULL

(22) Loch Spelve at Kinlochspelve – in this unusually pastoral setting for the Island of Mull, one is never without the company of sheep.

(23) This lonely cottage has a position it would be hard to better – at the head of Loch Scridain in south-western Mull, near Kilfinichen Bay.

(24) Summer sunshine on the countryside near Kilfinichen Bay on Loch Scridain. The loch runs eastward into Mull from the shore near Iona.

(25) From Kinloch at the head of Loch
Scridain, the mountains on the skyline are
(from left to right) Beinn nan Gubhar, Guibean
Uluvailt, and Corra-Bheinn.

(26) Thundery cloud hangs over the foreground while the sun illuminates the far head of Loch Scridain, with Corra-Bheinn in the distance.

(27) Lonely, fragile-looking trees like this one near Salen in the east of Mull are a common sight in the Scottish islands. Their isolation makes them vulnerable to the fierce winter gales.

(28) Rock formation and the shapes of the boulders can vary dramatically from one part of the island to another. These are at the edge of Loch na Keal on the west coast of Mull, near the island of Ulva.

(29) Mull abounds in fine waterfalls. This one tumbles over the cliff and plunges nearly 25 m into the blue waters of Loch Tuath below.

(30) Sheep often come to shelter from the weather by these small rocks on the shores of Loch Tuath.

(31) Eas Fors waterfall above Loch Tuath can be noisy enough in spring, when it is in spate, to make speech impossible.

(32) Eas Fors waterfall seen from below: this is a true cascade, falling over dozens of rock ledges before splashing to the shore of Loch Tuath.

(33) In some light, the surface of the loch waters can take on the silvery sheen of mercury. This picture of Loch Tuath was taken on a very grey day.

IONA

(34) Iona is a modest little island, yet it has a magnetic spiritual attraction that few can resist. The Abbey draws hundreds of thousands of visitors from all over the world.

COLL

(35) The Disney-like castle at Loch Breachacha is at the southern end of Coll. A farmhouse and two castles are the only buildings in this part of the island.

(36) This is the only inhabited dwelling at
Sorisdale, which is towards the northern tip of
Coll. For some, absence of electricity and
telephone represents an idyllic, desert-island
way of life!

SKYE

(37) This picture is taken from Knock Bay near
Armadale, in south-eastern Skye, looking
across the Sound of Sleat to the jagged peak of
Beinn Sgritheall on the mainland of Scotland.

(38) Peach-coloured marble, near Armadale.

(39) A chalk quarry nearby turns the waters
of Loch Slapin, in southern Skye, a delicate
turquoise.

(40) This little graveyard on the edge of Loch Cill Chriosd is tidily maintained, though the ruined church attached to it is no longer attended.

(41) Beinn na Cailleach looms up behind this old Celtic cross in the graveyard near Loch Cill Chriosd. Lowering skies add to the brooding atmosphere of the place.

(42) The waters of Loch Cill Chriosd are always thick with reeds and lilies, and herons abound here. In the background is Beinn na Cailleach. It and the hills round it are sometimes known as the Red Hills of Skye, and the next picture shows why.

(43) The reeds of Loch Cill Chriosd and the
slopes of Beinn na Cailleach glow red-gold in
the sunlight, giving rise to the sobriquet – 'The
Red Hills'.

(44) Summer flowers carpet the meadows near Broadford, with the Scottish mainland on the horizon beyond the Inner Sound.

_____

(45) Despite the threatening clouds overhead, brilliant sunshine illuminates the mass of wild flowers and the whitewashed cottage near Broadford, with Inner Sound as a backdrop.

(46) A crofter's cottage, abandoned, crouches beneath a sheer granite cliff at Elgol, rust-coloured lichen encrusting its roof.

(47) A single-track road leads to Elgol on its remote peninsula in south-western Skye. From here one can view the Cuillin mountains at their finest.

(48) 'The far Cuillin . . .' All too often the journey to Elgol for a view of these superb mountains is wasted because they are shrouded in mist. On a clear day, though, the view across Loch Scavaig is memorable.

(49) At the far end of Glen Brittle, on the
south-western coast of Skye, sheep
congregate, awaiting their shepherd.

(50) The River Brittle slides unobtrusively into the Sea of the Hebrides at Mussel Scalp Beach.

(51) On this very old crofter's cottage at Luib,
Loch Ainort, north of Broadford, the thatch is
secured by hanging stones.

(52) Allt Coire nam Bruadaran flows into Loch Ainort and is one of the many cascades to be seen on Skye. Violent in spring, it becomes gentler during summer.

(53) Nature takes a hold wherever she can –
this tree rooted in rock stands sentinel over the
narrows of Raasay, fifteen miles north of
Broadford.

(54) This picture is taken through drying fishing-nets, looking across Loch Sligachan to the Isle of Raasay.

(55) Autumnal colours and a turbulent sky
combined to make this atmospheric
photograph in Glen Drynoch, near Sligachan.

(56) Marsco is seen here from Sligachan. Both Marsco and Glamaig (next picture) rise up like pyramids, and their peaks are frequently veiled with low cloud.

(57) Glamaig (775 m above sea-level) can only be seen as an almost perfect pyramid from this viewpoint across the River Allt.

(58) Shafts of sunlight, piercing the clouds above Sligachan, illuminate this mountainous scene, with the cone of Glamaig on the far left.

(59) McQueen's Rock, a massive outcrop,
shelters Portree which lies to the north of it.
This picture is taken from Upper Ollach.

(60) The jutting pinnacle of the Old Man of Storr, most famous of the island's landmarks, is clearly seen in the distance against the pale sky. It attracts visitors from all over the world, and intrepid climbers have succeeded in scaling it.

(61) From the foot of the Old Man of Storr
there is a magnificent view across Loch
Leathan, which reflects sky and cloud like a
mirror.

(62) Staffin Bay, on the north-eastern coast of
Skye: the movement of water over sand results
in fascinating designs.

(63) The Quiraing is a group of weirdly shaped rocky outcrops in the very north of Skye. They are known as The Table, The Needle and The Prison.

(64) The splendid remains of Duntulm Castle are silhouetted against the golden glow of the setting sun. In the background are the still waters of Little Minch, and in the far distance the Outer Hebrides – Lewis and Harris.

(65) There is a small harbour at Meanish Pier
on Loch Pooltiel, which is on the western coast
of Skye.

(66) A rock masquerading as precious metal,
on the seashore at Skye.

NORTH UIST

(67) The Outer Hebrides are seamed and laced with water, as this photograph of the southern part of North Uist shows. Eaval in the distance stands 347 m high.

(68) Only a handful of crofters' cottages, like this one at Malaclete, still maintain their original thatch: most now have have modern roofing.

HARRIS

(69) Sheep will travel and graze anywhere, even on seemingly inaccessible islets. This photograph was taken near Rodel, at the southern tip of Harris.

(70) Loch Langavat, in southern Harris,
looking at Bleaval (some 398 m high) in the
rosy light of a winter evening.

(71) The mysterious pile of dark sand, contrasting with the colours beyond it, is simply builders' sand ready to be used in a new construction. In the background is the Sound of Taransay, looking to West Loch Tarbert.

(72) Subtle colouring and strong rock shapes
make a satisfying picture of this view across
the Sound of Taransay from Bay Steinigie.

(73) The pure white of the sand of Traigh Seilebost, and the vivid aquamarine of the sea, remind one of the tropics. In the distance are Ben Luskentyre and North Harris.

(74) At Meavaig, south of Tarbert on the eastern shore of Harris, the greyness of the light imparts a rather sinister feel to this small loch.

(75) Little cairns of peat turfs are a common sight on the Scottish islands, always perfectly stacked to dry, ready for winter. Every household relies on peat for its fire.

(76) A stack of peat turfs overlooks Loch
Ceann Dibig, south of Tarbert, on a still
summer afternoon.

(77) Above Glen Lingadale, just a little east of
Tarbert, are these rocks, whose strange
markings and precarious positioning often
leave visitors wondering.

(78) Traigh Luskentyre, looking towards
North Harris – this is more than a mere beach,
it is a huge expanse of sand left perfectly
smooth by the retreating sea.

(79) A tidal wave of cloud pours through the dip between Mulla-fo-dheas on the left and Clisham on the right, in this picture taken from Ardhasig, just north of Tarbert.

(80) Strangely, no house stands in front of this gate which looks south across West Loch Tarbert from Tolmachan.

(81) A *corps de ballet* of minute yellow flowers
tosses and sways in the strong wind that so
often gusts over the Outer Hebrides.

(82) Surprisingly, most of the Scottish islands
see snow only rarely, but ice and frost often
cover them for the coldest months, as can be
seen in this view from Maraig, north of
Tarbert.

LEWIS

(83) An extraordinary air of mystery surrounds these ancient standing stones at Callanish.

(84) In the evening stillness, Loch Croistean reflects distant Cleite Ghiosla and the soft colours of twilight.

(85) On Lewis's far western coast is a range of
hills, Mealisual (580 m) being the highest of
them. Beyond these there is nothing but the
vast Atlantic.